ADAM OF THE ROAD

by
Elizabeth Janet Gray

Teacher Guide

Written by
Monica L. Odle

Note
The Puffin Books paperback edition, © 1987, was used to prepare this guide. Page references may differ in other editions.
Novel ISBN: 0-14-032464-X

Please note: Please assess the appropriateness of this book for the age level and maturity of your students prior to reading and discussing it with them.

ISBN 1-58130-875-2

Printed in the United States of America.

To order, contact your local school supply store, or—

Novel Units, Inc.
P.O. Box 97
Bulverde, TX 78163-0097

Web site: www.novelunits.com

Lori Mammen, Editorial Director
Andrea M. Harris, Production Manager/Production Specialist
Suzanne K. Mammen, Curriculum Specialist
Heather Marnan, Product Development Specialist
Jill Reed, Product Development Specialist
Nancy Smith, Product Development Specialist
Adrienne Speer, Production Specialist

Table of Contents

Skills and Strategies

Thinking
Research, compare/contrast, analysis, creative thinking, critical thinking, evaluation, brainstorming, predicting, pros/cons, decision making

Writing
Poetry, letters, songs, Latin/English translations, character sketch

Listening/Speaking
Performance, drama, debate, listening, oral presentation, discussion

Vocabulary
Synonym/antonym, definitions, parts of speech, context clues, glossary

Comprehension
Cause/effect, story mapping

Literary Elements
Foreshadowing, conflict, figurative language, point of view, setting, theme, characterization

Across the Curriculum
History—crests, Middle Ages, feudalism, patronage, England, politics, education, religion, stories, "old wives' tales"; Art—design, collage, painting, sculpting, caricature; Geography—map reading, map making, England; Music—song writing, harp lessons; Foreign Language—Latin

Genre: historical fiction

Setting: thirteenth-century England

Point of View: third-person omniscient

Themes: loss, an individual's character, independence, adventure, family

Conflict: person vs. self, person vs. person, person vs. society

Tone: upbeat, informative

Summary

Life is a joy for Adam, Roger the minstrel's son. Then his beloved dog, Nick, is stolen, and Adam is separated from his father while pursuing the thief who took Nick. Adam uses his talents as a minstrel to make his way around England in search of his father, and he learns that the road truly is home to a minstrel. Along the way, his grand adventures teach him valuable lessons about character, benevolence, and the social order of his day.

About the Author

Elizabeth Janet Gray Vining was born in Pennsylvania on October 6, 1902. She married in her twenties, but her husband died in 1933, leaving her a widow. She became a professional writer and librarian. In 1942, she won the Newbery medal for *Adam of the Road.* After World War II, she was selected to tutor the 11-year-old crown prince of Japan, the future Emperor Akihito. She arrived in Japan in 1946 and remained there for four years, developing a close relationship with her pupil. Upon her return to the United States, she wrote a book entitled *Windows for the Crown Prince* (1952) about her time in Japan, and it became a bestseller. During her life, Vining wrote over 60 books. She died of natural causes on November 27, 1999, at age 97.

Characters

Adam Quartermayne: 11-year-old son of Roger the minstrel; travels around England in search of his father and his dog, Nick

Roger Quartermayne, a.k.a. Roger the minstrel: Adam's father; disappears in Guildford

Perkin: Adam's best friend at St. Alban's Abbey

Dame Malkin: widow woman who keeps Adam's dog for him while he is in school at St. Alban's

Sir Edmund de Lisle: Roger the minstrel's patron

Emilie de Lisle: Edmund's eldest daughter; heir to his estate

Margery de Lisle: Edmund's younger daughter; Adam's love interest

Hugh: Edmund's nephew; loves Adam's war horse, Bayard

William and Martin: sons of Edmund de Lisle's falconer

Matthew: son of Edmund de Lisle's bailiff

Agnes: Matthew's cousin; stays with the bailiff's family at Sir Edmund's home in London while the family is in Ludlow; disliked by both Matthew and Adam

Simon Talbot: one of Sir Edmund's young squires; in love with Emilie de Lisle; Adam's favorite squire

Jankin: minstrel to whom Roger loses Bayard in a dice game; steals Nick from Adam after laming Bayard

Dame Clarice: wife of the innkeeper at Burford Bridge

John and Jill Ferryman: young couple who help Adam when he first loses his father after swimming the river after Jankin and Nick

Daun William of Dover: merchant on his way to St. Giles' Fair; travels with Adam and is robbed by a knight

Sir Adam Gurdon: bailiff whom Adam finds to rescue Daun William

Sir Robert de Rideware: the robber knight who attacks Daun William's party

Master Walter: vicar of the parish in Winchester; keeps Adam after he falls on his head

Dame Prudence: Master Walter's sister; takes Adam's minstrel's coat and replaces it with a new one; cares for Adam while he is in Winchester

Jack de Vesey: husband and father of a family of struggling minstrels; poor but kind

Alison de Vesey: Jack's wife

Lawrence de Vesey: one of Jack's sons; steals food for the family to eat, forcing them to escape an arrest

Andrew de Vesey: unusually tall son of Jack; often borrows Adam's harp and ends up with it after the hue and cry

Wat: Perkin's father; a plowman

Gunnilda: Perkin's mother; makes Adam a new minstrel's coat and hat

Robin: Perkin's older brother; favors oxen over horses

Dickon: Perkin's younger brother; too young to help with the harvest

Background Information

Adam of the Road is set in what is known as the High Middle Ages of thirteenth-century England during the reign of King Edward I, also known as "Longshanks" because of his tall frame. During his reign, King Edward I conquered Wales and exercised great power over Scotland until his death. King Edward was greatly grieved by the death of his wife, Eleanor of Castile, in 1290, and had Eleanor crosses erected in each place that her funeral procession stopped for the night. These crosses are referenced in the novel. In 1295, King Edward called a Model Parliament, which was the first of its kind because it allowed representation not only from members of the aristocracy and the clergy, but also from counties and boroughs. He hoped to gain wider support to raise taxes to fund his wars, but the parliament never approved the proposed legislation.

Distinct classes and social hierarchies were crucial to the feudal society of the time. The aristocracy ruled over peasants, and marriage between social classes was very unusual. The feudal society began largely because of the need for protection from robbers and other criminals who roamed the land. Commoners sold their homes and freedom to lords in exchange for protection. Lords were warriors, and they highly valued the protection of their estates and families and lived primarily in castles and fortresses. Their estates were not only made up of serfs who worked the land, but also of clergy, bards, minstrels, and other servants. Chivalry to ladies was also highly valued in this era.

The minstrels of the thirteenth century were the paid entertainers—they could sing, dance, perform acrobatics or magic, juggle, and play many instruments. Some minstrels had patron lords, but not all. Minstrels with the benefit of a patron had more protection and more financial security than those without a patron lord. Those with patrons were able to benefit from the protection of their lord's estate, but did not live there the entire year. When their services were not needed, they would often travel to fairs and other events seeking out people to entertain. They told stories of historical heroes, romances, poetry, tales, and fables, and sang lyrical songs. At times, minstrels were also called upon to join their lord in battle, providing music for the regiments or playing the trumpet during battle. Minstrels without a patron had no place to call their own. They roamed the streets looking for new people to entertain and were worse off than the lowest of peasants, who at least had a form of protection and a plot of land to sow. Church leaders tended to oppose the work of the minstrels, taking offense at some minstrels' impersonations of religious figures, lude gestures, and indecent exposure in the name of entertainment. By the fourteenth century, opposition to minstrels was less harsh, though the church still opposed forms of entertainment they believed led to excess and sin.

Initiating Activities

1. Prediction: Look at the front cover and the map at the beginning of the book and discuss what students think the book will be about. Why is the book titled *Adam of the Road*?
2. History: Research thirteenth-century England and its feudal society. What is feudalism? Describe the social hierarchy of that time.
3. Brainstorming: Write the phrase "Medieval Entertainment" in the center oval on the Attribute Web (page 7 of this guide). Have students brainstorm what people in medieval times might have done for entertainment.
4. Prediction: Ask students if they have ever read a book of historical fiction. As a class, predict how much of the story will portray reality and how much will be fiction. Discuss how to tell the difference between fact and fiction.
5. Social Studies/Research: Learn about the role of the Catholic Church in thirteenth-century England. As a class, discuss specific aspects of the Catholic faith such as pilgrimages, saints, and miracle plays, which will appear in the novel.

Vocabulary Activities

1. Word Sort: Assign students 20 vocabulary words. Have students sort the words into different categories, including verbs, nouns, adverbs, and adjectives.
2. Word Quilt: Have students create a word quilt. Each student chooses a vocabulary word from the book. Using different colors of paper, the students create unique squares to represent the words they chose, including one square each for the definition, part of speech, pronunciation, a synonym, an antonym, an illustration, and a quote from the book. Finally, have students paste the squares together on a larger square sheet of paper. Display the word quilts in the classroom.
3. Sentence-by-Sentence: With the class, come up with a sentence to start a story. Have students pass around one sheet of paper with the starter-sentence at the top. Each student must add one sentence to the story. Each sentence must correctly use one vocabulary word. After each class member has had a chance to contribute to the story, allow a volunteer to read the story aloud.
4. Unfamiliar Word List: Have students flip through the book and select three words that they have never seen before or for which they do not know the definition. Students should look up these words and define them (as they are used in the book). Then they should write a unique sentence for each word that demonstrates its definition. Collect the words from the students. Make a master list of the unfamiliar words and their definitions. Hand out copies of this list to the students.

5. Synonym/Antonym Race: Randomly select 20 vocabulary words. Give each student a list of the words. The first student to correctly identify either a synonym or antonym for each word, as it is used in the text, is the winner.
6. Glossary: Encourage students to keep a list of any unfamiliar or difficult words they encounter while reading the novel. As an extra-credit assignment, have students create a glossary from their list. Glossaries should include the part of speech and definition of each word as it is used in the novel.

Attribute Web

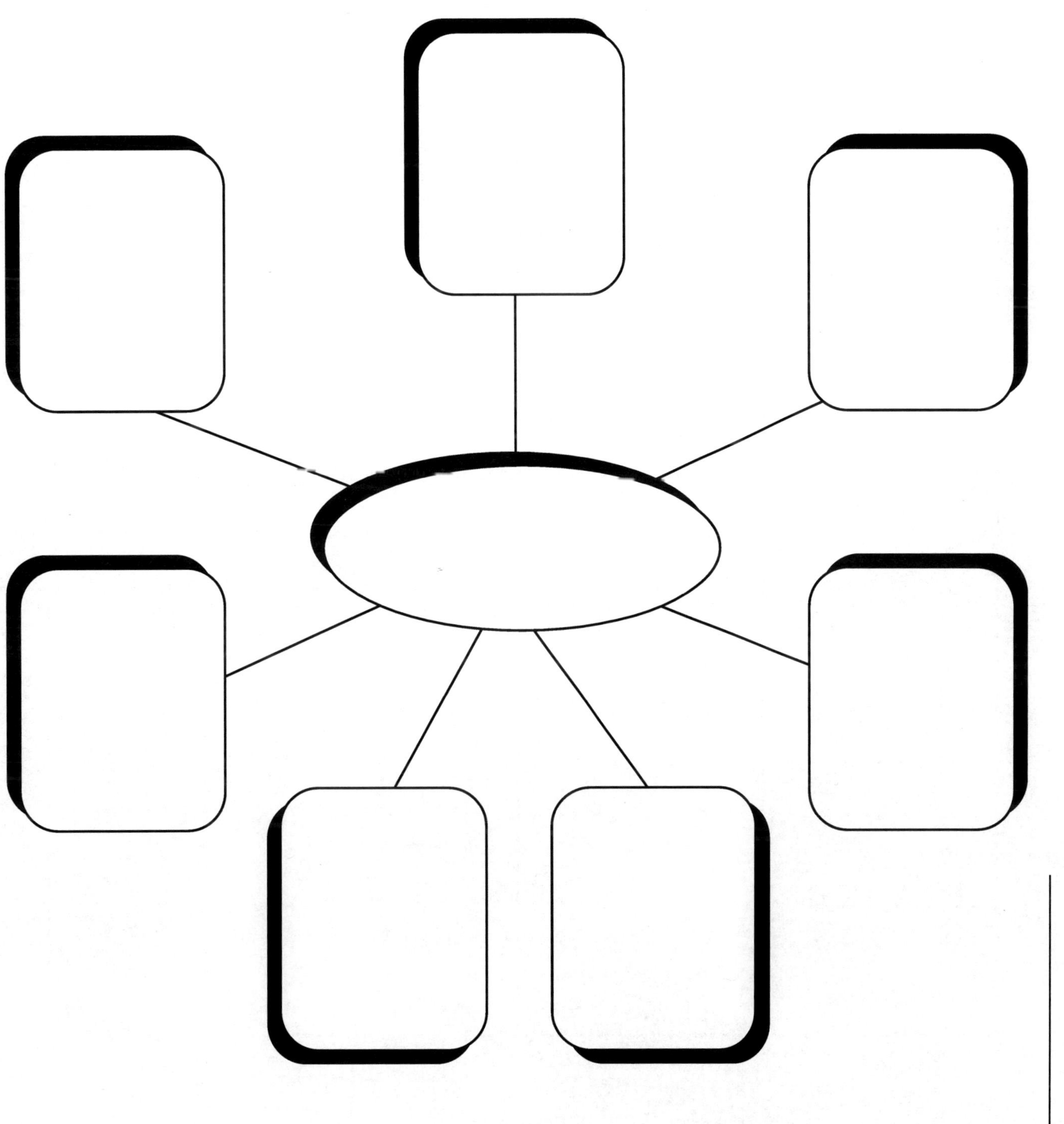

Prediction Chart

What characters have we met so far?	What is the conflict in the story?	What are your predictions?	Why did you make these predictions?

Character Web

Directions: Complete the attribute web by filling in information specific to a character in the book.

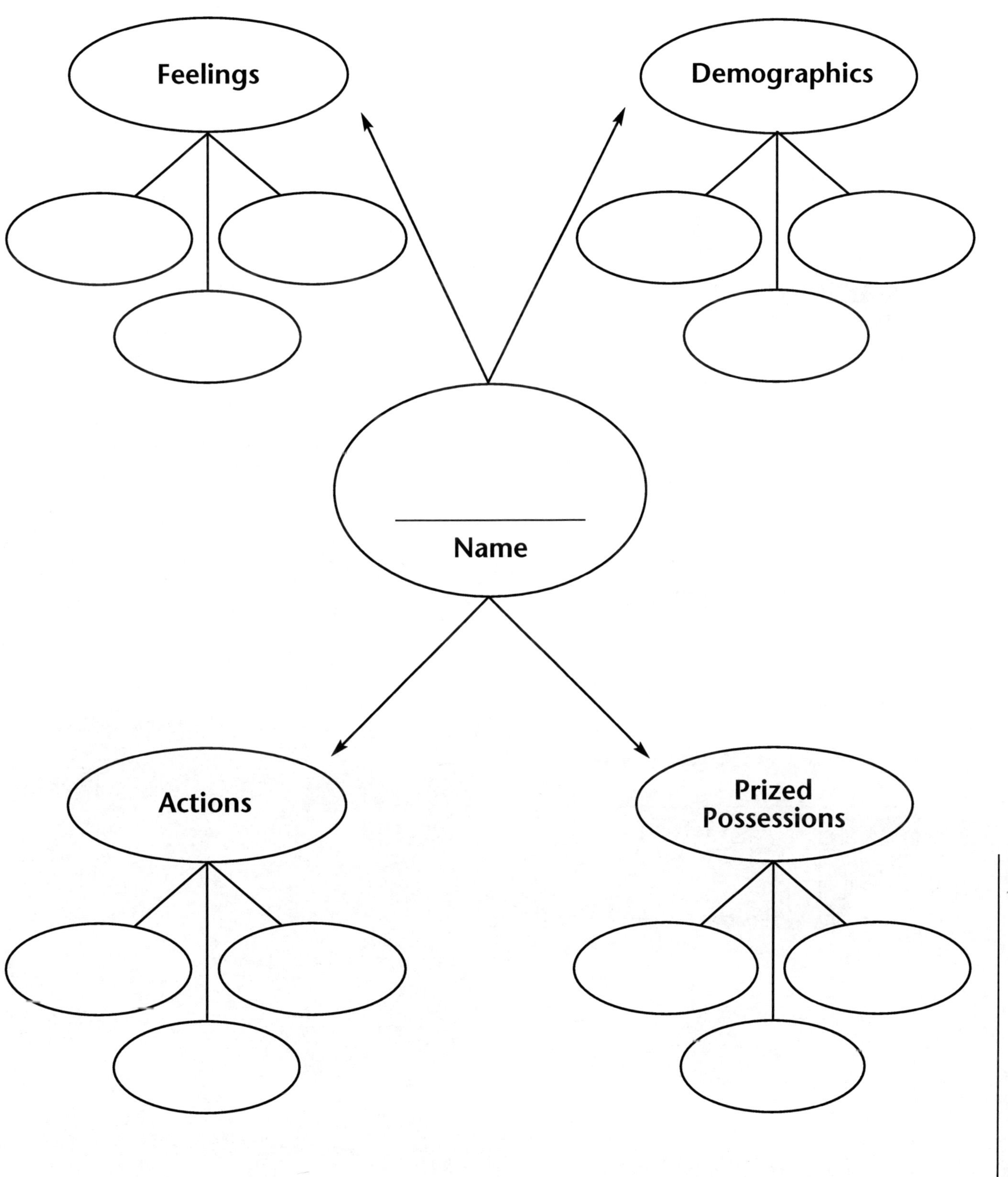

Story Map

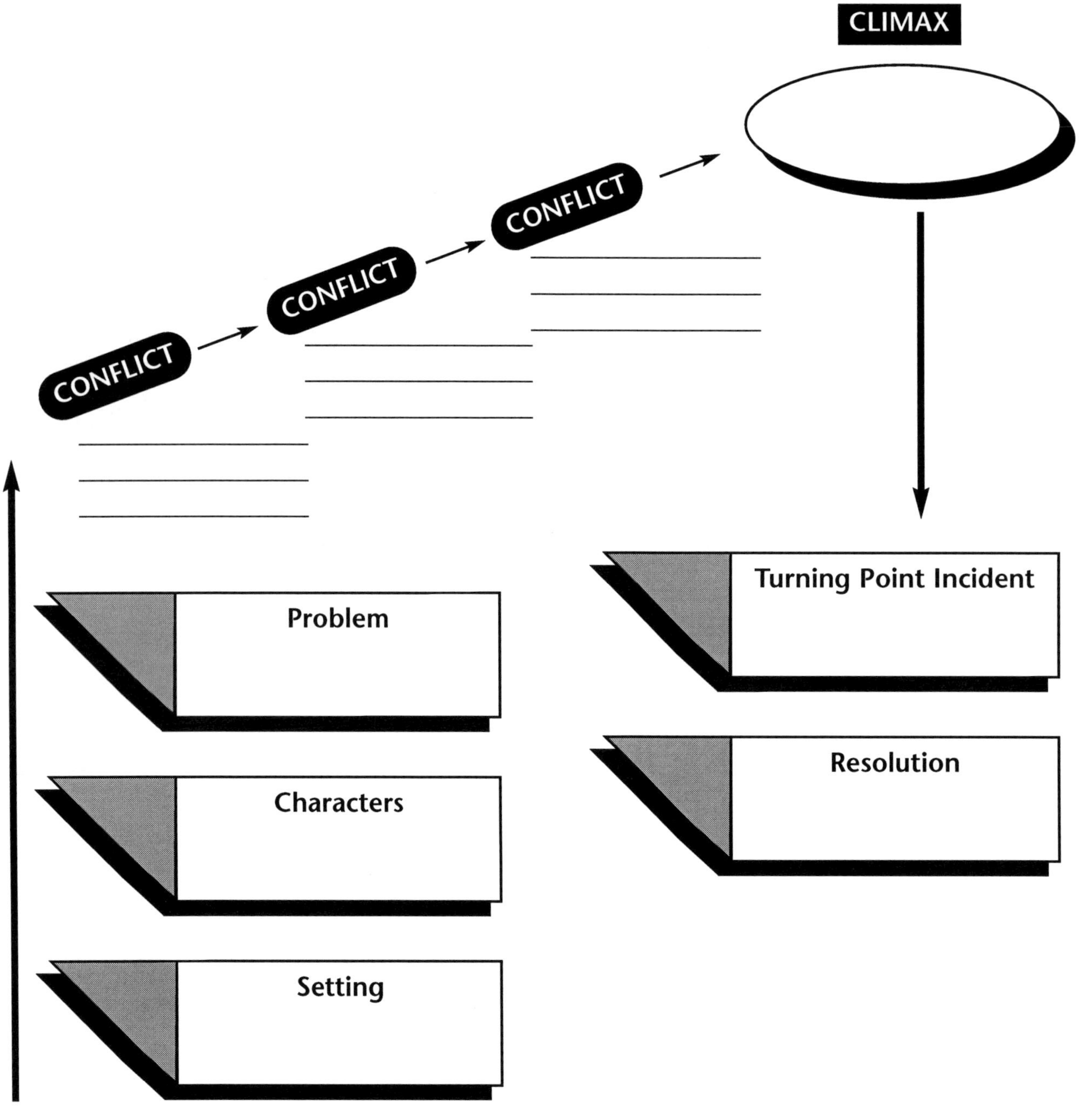

CLIMAX
CONFLICT
CONFLICT
CONFLICT
Turning Point Incident
Problem
Resolution
Characters
Setting

Foreshadowing Chart

Foreshadowing is the literary technique of giving clues to coming events in a story.

Directions: What examples of foreshadowing do you recall from the story? If necessary, skim through the chapters to find examples of foreshadowing. List at least four examples below. Explain what clues are given, then list the coming event that is suggested.

Foreshadowing	Page #	Clues	Coming Event

Feelings

Directions: Complete the chart below.

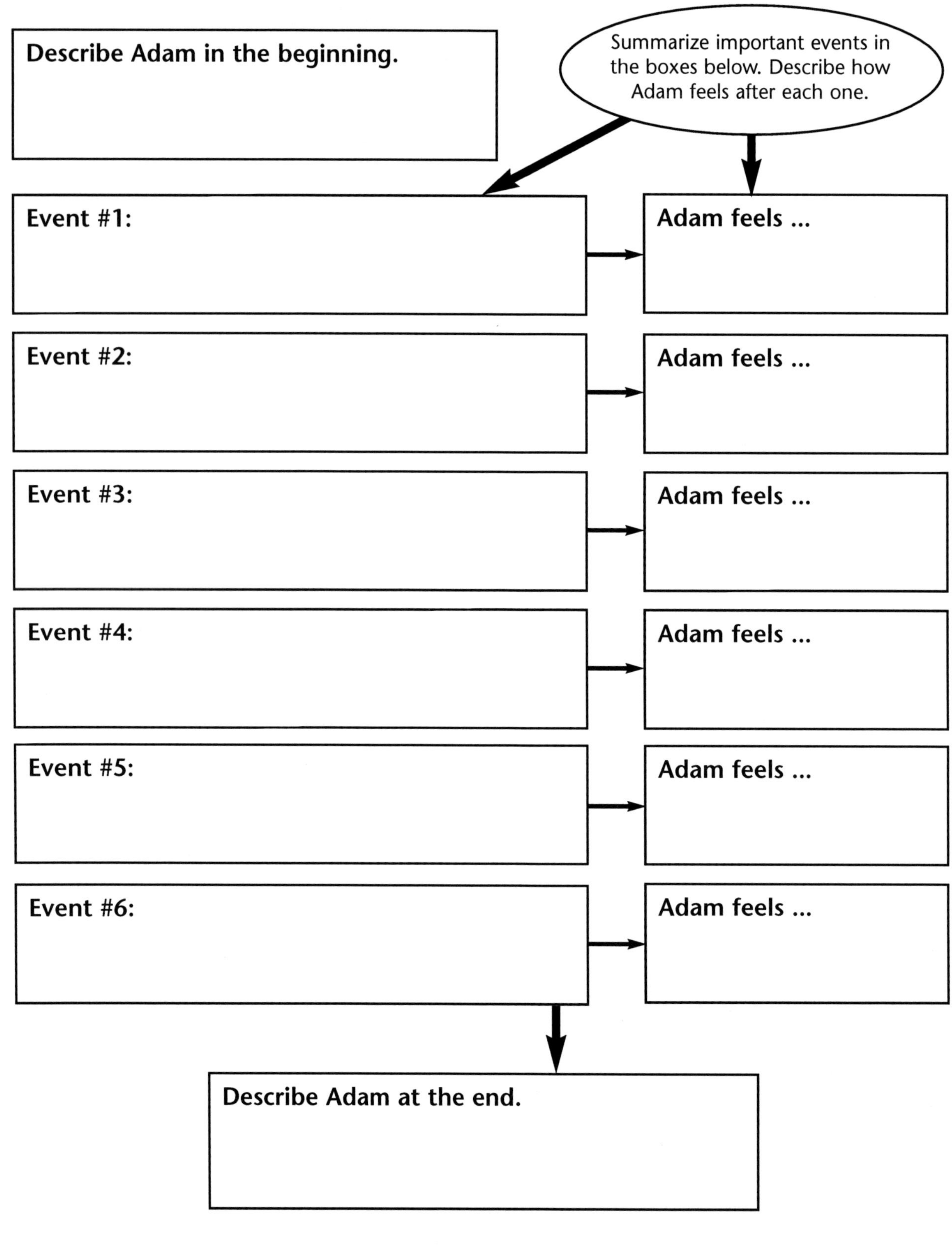

Chapters 1–6, pp. 11–80

Adam is tired of school at St. Alban's Abbey and eagerly anticipates the return of his father, Roger the minstrel. Adam enjoys playing his harp, spending time with his friend Perkin, and visiting his dog Nick, who stays with a widow near the school property. After Roger returns, he, Adam, and Nick travel with Sir Edmund de Lisle, Roger's new patron. The other young boys who travel with the de Lisle family eventually befriend Adam after he shares his father's war horse, Bayard, with them.

Vocabulary

dormitory (13)
minstrel (13)
surcoat (14)
interludes (14)
abbot (15)
refrains (16)
fabliaux (16)
parish (16)
dwindling (18)
porter (21)
coif (22)
almonry (23)
dole (23)
carp (24)
tuft (24)
disdain (28)
plaintive (29)
hillock (35)
heraldic (36)
gilded (37)
rotary (39)
sober (40)
portmanteau (45)
sulkily (48)
impudently (49)
succession (55)
muffled (56)
guise (59)
oyster (63)
lay (65)
rushes (66)
tiltyard (69)
mettlesome (71)
lanneret (71)
quintain (73)
jennet (74)
yeomen (77)
mews (78)
lithe (78)

Discussion Questions

1. What kind of person is Adam's father, Roger the minstrel? *(He is an intelligent minstrel who is favored by the upper classes of Britain. Adam sees his father as a gallant figure with a very reputable occupation, and he wants to be just like him. pp. 13–15)*

2. What kind of person is Perkin? Contrast Perkin with Adam. *(Perkin is an intelligent boy, the son of a plowman. With many people working hard to make Perkin's education possible, Perkin is a serious student intent on fulfilling his dream of being a legal counselor to the king. Adam is at the school because he could not accompany his father to France, and spends his days waiting for his father's return. Education is not as important to Adam as it is to Perkin. Adam's presence in Perkin's life causes Perkin to become more lighthearted. pp. 17–18)*

3. Describe the Abbey of St. Alban. *(It is like a city, full of people and many kinds of trades. Poor and rich, monks and lay people, nobles and servants all work together in the community. The abbey church sits at the center of the "city." p. 23)*

4. As Adam joins the de Lisle party with Roger, what indications are there of the different social classes of the travelers? *(Answers will vary. Note Hugh's distinguished air, indicating he is of noble blood. Also, the women traveling in a carriage are evidence of Edmund de Lisle's wealth. Because it is unusual for Roger, a simple minstrel who usually has no horse, to have been given a fine war horse, it shows that he is well esteemed in the eyes of his patron. At the tiltyard, the roles the boys play [yeomen, knights, etc.] mimic their actual social status. throughout)*

5. What does Roger say about the road? Does this help you better understand the title of the book? What do you predict will happen in the rest of the story with regard to the road? *(Roger says the road is a holy thing that should be properly cared for because it brings people all over England together. He also says the road is the minstrel's home. Answers and predictions will vary. p. 52)*

6. What does Roger mean when he says, "Green apples ripen in time" (p. 65)? *(that Adam is young and still has things to learn; His mistakes with his harp are due to his youth, as is his departure from the carriage without any polite, parting words.)*

7. How does Adam behave around the blush of boys in the tiltyard? What does he learn about Hugh? How does this affect

the way he sees Hugh? *(Answers will vary. Note that at first Adam pines away for attention from the boys, but then remembers he can ride Bayard. After sharing Bayard with the others, he learns that Hugh loves Bayard as he [Adam] loves Nick. This helps Adam understand why Hugh was not kind to him earlier and is more eager to be his friend now. pp. 71–75)*

8. Compare and contrast the way the boys see education in the book and the way education is viewed in American culture today. *(In both times, education is important, but the type of education one values is different. In the Middle Ages, people were educated for a specific trade or lifestyle, which usually followed the trade or lifestyle of their father or family. A general education at school was not widely valued, except by those who needed education to advance their sphere of life [such as Perkin]. Today, America considers general education as a right to all of its citizens, and government money is spent to make sure every person is able to receive a fair and equal education. Specialized education is almost nonexistent in public schools until students are in their last years of high school, or in a college or trade school after they receive their high school diploma. pp. 77–78)*

Supplementary Activities

1. Figurative Language: Keep a list of figurative language the author uses in the book. Continue adding to the list as you read. Examples: **Similes**—"brushed the coif...as if it had been a fly" (p. 22); "sound as doleful as a hen in the snow" (p. 29); "you're as pert as a pie" (p. 30); "carriage...shaped like an enormous sausage" (p. 37); "motes danced...like golden rain" (p. 45); "blue eyes like bits of glass" (p. 47); "Adam's heart softened and spread like butter in the sun" (p. 47); "Roger's voice...like music" (p. 58) **Metaphors**—Nick: red whirlwind (p. 26); Adam: oyster (p. 63); Adam: green apple (p. 65) **Personification**—"brown eyes swam with tears" (p. 59); "harp...said nasally" (p. 60)
2. History: Research the role of minstrels in the Middle Ages. Write a report about their duties and their place in society. If possible, draw a picture of a minstrel in a traditional minstrel's outfit to accompany your report.
3. History/Art: Look for pictures of different abbeys located throughout England. On a piece of poster board, display different pictures of abbeys. You can draw your own or use copies of pictures you find in your resources. Identify the different pictures to help educate people who view your display about abbey life.
4. History/Oral Interpretation: On page 69, the author refers to three stories about friendship in medieval times. Research one of the three stories—"The Song of Roland," "The History of Damon and Pythias," or "The Adventures of Horn"—and tell part of the story to your class.

Chapters 7–9, pp. 81–121

Adam continues to enjoy Hugh's company. After Emilie de Lisle's wedding, Roger, Adam, and Nick leave on foot for St. Giles' Fair. They encounter Jankin while eating and later at an inn where Roger performs the tale of King Horn. Jankin wins Bayard from Roger during a dice game, but has lamed Bayard by riding him too hard, which delays his travels. Roger, Adam, and Nick sleep at the inn, and Adam unknowingly says goodbye to Nick before he falls asleep.

Vocabulary

wherry (83)
rancid (83)
mutton (83)
parchment (84)
vestments (88)
psalteries (89)
summoned (90)
apprentice (96)
transacting (99)
gesticulating (99)
perpetual (100)
subsidy (100)
garth (101)
glutton (102)
wharf (104)
gradual (112)
distaff (114)
spindle (114)
proverb (115)
duress (116)
chapman (118)
hesitated (120)

Discussion Questions

1. What ironies are depicted regarding the role of women in the Middle Ages as Hugh and Adam discuss Emilie's marriage? *(Hugh says that women must do as they are told and that it doesn't matter what Emilie wants to do or whom she wants to marry. Because she is Sir Edmund's only heir, she must protect the estate by marriage. This is ironic to Adam because he sees the young boys attending to Margery's every desire and seeking to please her with their chivalry and gallant acts when they pretend that she is their liege lady. On one hand, the woman is to be cherished, pleased, and delighted. On the other, she is to obey orders, even in the selection of a husband, for marriage is a political enterprise and not an extension of a loving relationship. pp. 83–85)*

2. What does Roger receive for his work at the wedding? What does he do with his earnings? *(He is given a brooch in the shape of a popular quatre-foil from Emilie. Sir Edmund gives him, along with the other minstrels, a bag of silver pennies. Roger plays dice and loses all of his money and Bayard to a minstrel named Jankin. pp. 90–92)*

3. How is the atmosphere of London different from that at Sir Edmund's? *(London is more crowded and dirty. It smells of trash, and animals wander freely. Because some buildings are so high, the sun doesn't shine on some of the streets. The city is also a place where people trade and do business, such as on Paul's Walk, an actual road that went through the center of St. Paul's Cathedral in the Middle Ages. p. 98)*

4. What does Sir Edmund give Roger before he goes? Why is this important to Roger? *(a parchment commending Roger's talents to any of his friends; Sir Edmund asks that those who partake of Roger's services give him a subsidy, or payment, which Roger now greatly needs after losing his money to Jankin. Later, it is also evident that such a letter will give Roger passage into manors that others would not be permitted to enter. p. 100)*

5. How does Roger feel about Jankin? about gambling? How do you know? *(Answers will vary. Note how Roger does not seem pleased to see Jankin at the restaurant. He also emphatically declares he will no longer play dice. Because of his sad mood, students may infer that he regrets playing dice with Jankin and losing his money and Bayard. He does not answer Adam's question about whether or not Jankin will ride Bayard to death, which could mean he also thinks Jankin will take poor care of the horse. His abrupt ending to the meal where Jankin joins them, and his reluctance to tell Jankin where they are headed, could mean that he does not like Jankin. pp. 96–97, 103–105)*

6. Why do Adam and Roger decide to tell the tale of King Horn at the inn? Why do you think Roger lets Adam decide what to tell? *(Adam is tired of all the love stories about romance and*

chivalry. He also decides French stories would not be welcome at an inn, where nobles are unlikely to stay. Answers will vary. By allowing Adam to think through the process of selecting a tale, Roger is training Adam to make such decisions when he becomes a minstrel one day. pp. 111–112)

7. How does Roger ask for payment from the people at the inn? In our culture, what is comparable to a minstrel? *(He stops in mid-sentence and asks for money to continue the tale. Answers will vary. Students may compare minstrels to actors, musicians, or even circus performers. p. 120)*
8. **Prediction:** What will happen to Nick? Why do you think so?

Supplementary Activities

1. Figurative Language: **Similes**—"voice like a trumpet" (p. 85); "minstrels...attracted to a feast like flies to honey" (p. 89); "tall and gaunt as a tree" (p. 91); "She flung out orders like blows" (p. 113); "bright as glass" (p. 119); "Your tale limps like your horse" (p. 120)
2. Language/Translation: On page 101, Adam says something about Nick in Latin: "egregium instrionem et eius egregium canem." Translate what Adam says into English.
3. History: On pages 115–117, an old man at the inn tells Adam what led to King John signing the "Great Charter" or the Magna Carter at Runnymede in 1215. Research this historic event and write two to three paragraphs explaining its significance to the English people.
4. Prediction: Begin the Prediction Chart on page 8 of this guide.

Chapters 10–13, pp. 123–173

Adam awakens at the inn to find that Jankin has stolen Nick. Roger and Adam leave quickly to follow Jankin to Guildford. At Guildford, Adam spies Jankin and Nick in an alley and begins to chase them. After swimming across a river, Adam is exhausted and falls into a deep sleep. Upon awakening the next morning at the home of John and Jill Ferryman, he realizes he lost Roger in his zeal to follow Jankin. He travels to Guildford to look for Roger, but cannot find him. He then travels toward Farnham, where Roger and Jankin are both headed. Adam travels with a merchant who is attacked by a band of thieves, including a knight. Adam escapes the ambush and leaves to find the sheriff.

Vocabulary

obligingly (125)
hustled (126)
sullenly (127)
gist (128)
harbored (129)
poultice (129)
implored (130)
ingots (130)
cavalcade (133)
chaffed (134)
perils (139)
balky (141)
plodded (144)
babble (145)
looming (155)
beckoned (157)
fresco (159)
musingly (164)
daintily (165)
laden (167)
decreed (168)
menacingly (169)
unsheathe (169)
astride (172)
scabbard (172)
resolutely (173)

Discussion Questions

1. How does Adam respond when he finds out about Nick? Why can't Roger find words when he wants to speak to Adam about perils that sometimes come to boys and dogs? *(Adam first searches for Nick on his own, though he knows it will do no good. Then he leaves with Roger to look for someone who may have seen Jankin and a red spaniel. All along the way, Adam is zealous and impatient in the pursuit of his dog. Answers will vary. Roger wants to help Adam understand that hardship is often part of life, but he feels that telling Adam about life's injustices would be too difficult in that moment. He is overcome by Adam's optimism of finding Jankin and Nick and seems unwilling to damper Adam's hopeful spirit. pp. 126–145)*
2. Evaluate Adam's decision to run after Jankin and swim the river. What would you have done in his situation? *(Note that Adam does not make sure that Roger sees where he is headed when he begins to chase Jankin. Also note that he is so excited to see Nick that he is hesitant to wait for Roger, though he does call out to his father. Consider that after swimming the river, Adam was not much farther ahead of the ferry, especially because the river current had carried him downstream a bit. Also note that, having never traveled this way before, Adam would have been unfamiliar with the river current and the speed it would take to swim the river's width. In the end, he may have had more energy had he waited for the ferry, which would have allowed him to chase Jankin more effectively once he was on the opposite riverbank. Answers will vary. pp. 141–149)*
3. Why is the woman who finds Adam asleep on her dog horrified when she finds he slept the night before at Burford Bridge? *(She is probably amazed because he has traveled an incredibly long way in one day. She knows he must be exhausted, especially after swimming the river. p. 151)*
4. What advice does Jill Ferryman give Adam when she discovers he has lost his father? Do you agree or disagree with her advice? *(that his father is probably still in Guildford looking for him; She thinks if Adam returns to Guildford, he will find his father and they can travel to Farnham together to find Jankin, who will likely stay in Farnham a few days, thinking he has escaped Adam. Answers will vary. pp. 152–153)*

5. Why doesn't Adam enjoy his night at the castle? *(The people there are not very cheerful, and part of the castle is used as a jail so guards clank around everywhere. Though sharing a bed with the kind porter, Adam has to endure an evening of snoring, clinging uncomfortably to the edge of the bed so as not to disturb the bed's owner. p. 159)*
6. When at the inn in Farnham, what makes Adam remember being six years old? What does this memory reveal about his character? *(The merchant Adam knows at the inn speaks of his own son, who is six years old. Adam recalls being with his mother at age six, partly because the man is talking about a six year old, and possibly also because he feels lost and begins thinking about the people who love him and who he has now lost—both his mother and father. Through this memory, readers learn that Adam's mother passed away while he was young, but that she loved him and taught him to read and sing. Answers will vary. pp. 165–166)*
7. What happens to Adam in the king's woods? How does he respond? *(Adam and the merchant party are attacked by robbers, led by a knight with a leopard on his crest. Adam joins the other men in his party by yelling that they are being robbed until he realizes that he is free. Adam escapes the robbers, though he loses his harp, and hides in a tree until they leave. He then travels to the nearest town to find a sheriff. pp. 168–173)*

Supplementary Activities

1. Figurative Language: **Similes**—"his hands were soft and plump like little pink pigs" (p. 129); "thoughts and feelings buzzed like angry bees" (p. 132); "arms and legs felt like lead...like knives" (p. 145); "thought of Nick jabbed him like an arrow" (p. 145); "stretching out his neck like a rooster" (p. 170); "tree arching its branches like a green tent" (p. 171); "[boy] gone to earth like a fox" (p. 172) **Personification**—"timber clinging to the steep sides" (p. 140); "every minute that crawled slowly by" (p. 159)
2. Geography: Look at the map at the beginning of the book (pp. 2–3). Draw your own version of the part of the map that is discussed in this section. Highlight the path that Adam takes and try to estimate how many miles he travels until the robbers interrupt his journey.

Chapters 14–17, pp. 175–231

Adam finds Sir Adam the bailiff and tells him about the robbers. He travels with the bailiff's party to show them where the robbery took place and accompanies them to Sir de Rideware's house. Adam finds his harp, Daun William repacks his goods, and they resume their travels to Winchester. Adam begins his search for Roger at the fair, but is unsuccessful. He falls off a parish wall while watching a miracle play called *The Fall of Adam* and is taken in by the vicar of the parish and his sister. He stays with them until he learns that Roger challenged Jankin at the Court of the Dusty Feet for Nick, lost his case, and was told to leave Winchester. Adam leaves Winchester with the de Vesey family, a poor family of minstrels, to head for London in his continued search for Roger.

Vocabulary

demesne (179)
tarried (180)
scythes (180)
sheaves (180)
reeve (181)
yield (182)
blazoned (183)
palfrey (183)
sparser (185)
siege (185)
reedy (186)
disdainful (186)
resentful (189)
fretted (194)
lay (196)
palmer (203)
merit (204)
sapling (211)
indignation (211)
delved (213)
culmination (213)
serenity (218)
wimple (218)
vigorously (219)
gossamer (222)
tabor (227)

Discussion Questions

1. Why is the shepherd's joke about Adam's name nothing new to Adam? What does the joke mean? *(According to the Bible, Adam is the name of the first man God created. He lived in a beautiful garden called Eden until he ate an apple, which was the only fruit God had forbidden him to eat. Because of Adam's disobedience [sin], he was forced to leave Eden. In Adam Quartermayne's time, Bible stories were a significant part of the culture, and many people knew the story of Adam, so it would not be surprising if other people had made a joke about his name. pp. 178–179)*

2. What does it mean that the people in the village were doing "'boon work' that each villein was required to give to his lord" (p. 180)? What does this say about the culture of that time? *(Answers will vary. Note that this is a reference to feudalism. In a feudalistic society, workers were not slaves, but were bound to their master's land. They could work the land for themselves, but also had to work the land for the lord who owned the property. At harvest time, workers had to harvest the lord of the manor's crop before they could touch their own. This is one indicator that the story takes place in medieval times. It also shows how one's social rank can affect his daily activities. pp. 180–181)*

3. On his first night in Winchester, Adam sleeps at Strangers' Hall and overhears a political discussion. What are your opinions about the inferences the people make? Does it surprise you to hear some of this talk from people of the lower classes? How do you account for their loyalty to the king but not to the churchmen and nobles? *(Answers will vary. Note that it is easy for the poor to see how much money they give to the government contrasted with the lack of power they wield to make decisions or laws in the government. Students may compare this situation with modern society. For example, some people with little money may favor a specific president, but still complain about Congress or local leaders levying taxes on them. pp. 197–199)*

4. Do you consider Adam a person of faith? Why or why not? *(Answers will vary. Note that Adam stayed at St. Alban's Abbey to receive some education, and he also finds himself in the vicar's care. At St. Alban's, his stories did not always offend the overseers, so they allowed him to tell and sing many of his lays. He also goes to the shrine of St. Swithin to ask for a miracle when he cannot find Roger and Nick. [Students may debate about this act—that it is truly based on faith*

in the power of the saint or that it is a desperate last resort and not an act of faith.] However, note that the church generally disapproves of the minstrel's trade, and that Adam finds himself in conflict with Master Walter over the types of songs he can sing and tales he can tell. It does not seem that Adam has a strong devotion or faith based on what the narrator tells us of his journey. throughout)

5. What is ironic about the title of the play Adam watches in the courtyard? *(It is entitled* The Fall of Adam, *and after watching Adam and Eve "fall" as God removes them from Paradise, Adam Quartermayne falls from the wall on which he is sitting to view the play.)*
6. On page 225, Master Walter tells Adam not to sing or tell stories because of something St. Paul said to Timothy. He is referring to I Timothy 4:7 which says, "Have nothing to do with godless myths and old wives' tales; rather, train yourself to be godly" (NIV). Do you agree or disagree with the way Master Walter interprets this verse as he speaks to Adam? Why? *(Answers will vary. Note that mythology and old wives' tales often speak of a religion or superstition of their own. Consider this as students compare the types of stories Adam tells to the types of stories described in this verse.)*
7. How does Adam behave while staying at the parish? Do you approve or disapprove of the way Adam treats the vicar and his sister? Do you approve or disapprove of the way the vicar and his sister treat Adam? Why? *(Answers will vary. Consider that Adam is obedient and polite, and that he does what they ask of him. He is grateful for their kindness and treats them with respect, even though it means sacrificing something that he loves—playing his own songs and telling his own stories. However, he does not tell them in person when he chooses to leave, though he does send a note by messenger. Consider that the vicar and his sister do what they think is best for Adam, even though he does not agree. pp. 221–225, 231)*
8. Consider what the woman tells Adam as she tries to predict what Roger would have done after losing his case at the Court of the Dusty Feet. Do you agree or disagree with her speculations? Why? *(Answers will vary. pp. 228–229)*
9. **Prediction:** What will happen as Adam travels to London with the de Vesey family?

Supplementary Activities

1. Figurative Language: **Similes**—"Like ice forming in sudden swift splinters over a puddle, fear jabbed Adam's heart" (p. 202); "feed...you as if you were a baby robin" (p. 219); "howl like a baby" (p. 219); "gossamer lay on the grass like fairy washing spread out to dry" (p. 222)
Personification—"manor house...sleepy" (p. 183); "shouts...beat about his head" (p. 201); "mind went tramping over the white tracks" (p. 220)
2. Creative Writing: Write the dialogue, as if from a court reporter's records, of a case that might have been taken to the Court of the Dusty Feet during St. Giles' Fair in Winchester. Consider the types of people at the fair and the types of goods being sold as you write the dialogue.
3. Writing/Drama: Write a character sketch of Adam. Discuss what motivates Adam's behavior in specific incidents in the story, such as when he finds himself bragging after the knight robber is captured or when he finds himself in the care of the parish vicar.
4. History/Religion: Several saints are mentioned in Chapter 15. Select a Catholic saint and research the saint's history. Write one to two paragraphs explaining why the person was selected for sainthood and what the person symbolizes.

Chapters 18–20, pp. 233–276

Adam travels with the de Veseys until they steal food and are chased. He loses the de Veseys and his harp getting away from the authorities. He makes his way to London where he finds the de Lisle home. He discovers that Roger is not there, but has accompanied Sir Edmund to Wales and will probably not be back for Adam until May. Adam spends Christmas at the house with the bailiff and his family and soon after sees Jankin. Jankin tells him that he lost Nick a few weeks before, and Adam thinks that Nick returned to Dame Malkin's house.

Vocabulary

winnowing (235)
unscrupulous (238)
venison (240)
imperatively (241)
sinister (245)
levied (247)
burgesses (247)
morosely (256)
minted (259)
forlornly (267)
derisive (269)
quaver (270)
skeptically (271)
propelled (273)
vicinity (275)
glowered (275)

Discussion Questions

1. Compare and contrast Roger Quartermayne and Jack de Vesey. Consider whether the two statements on page 238 are the same or different: "You have to give people what they want" and "A minstrel must fit his tale to his listeners." *(Note that both men are minstrels with a family to support, and both have a child/children who are also minstrels. Consider that Roger was trained in France and speaks French, allowing him to cater to upper classes, while Jack has little means to be taught new tales from far away places. No patron supports Jack, but Roger has Sir Edmund as a patron. Having a patron also means that Roger has a letter to give to people while he travels, accrediting his abilities as a minstrel and persuading people to allow him into their homes. Jack has no such recommendation. There is also a difference in the tales the de Veseys tell and those that Roger tells—while Roger's tales appeal to his audiences' good natures, Jack's tales tend to entertain based on the mocking of others. Answers will vary. pp. 237–238, throughout)*
2. Do you think people who are hungry and poor should be allowed to hunt in the king's forest? *(Answers will vary. pp. 239–240)*
3. Discuss whether or not it was right for Lawrence to steal food. Consider the family's hunger as well as any other options they might have had to obtain something to eat. *(Answers will vary. Note that the family chooses not to ask the parson for any food, even though Adam insists that Master Walter gave food to any hungry person who came to his door. Also discuss the sensation of hunger, and have students imagine how they would feel if they traveled by foot from town to town eating nothing more than small pieces of bread. pp. 241–243)*
4. Why do you think Adam is so fond of the story about Havelok as he waits for daybreak under the bridge? *(The story is about a young man who is hungry and cold but is eventually recognized for who he truly is, and his sorrow is turned to joy. The situation could be compared, in some ways, to Adam's. While Adam is not a king, he is a minstrel who has not been able to act as a true minstrel since he lived with Master Walter and traveled with the de Veseys. pp. 251–253)*
5. Discuss how Adam feels after reaching the de Lisle house, not finding his father, and not having hope of seeing him for five more months. How would you feel in Adam's place? *(Answers will vary, but will probably address being disappointed, lonely, or even feeling abandoned or forgotten. Also point out that at least at the home of his father's patron, Adam will have plenty of food and a place to sleep. pp. 266–268)*
6. Compare and contrast Adam's holiday season with your own. Note the specific traditions and events the author includes in the novel to explain how people celebrated in thirteenth-century England. *(Answers will vary. Students may particularly notice Adam's lack of presents,*

but note how presents are exchanged on New Year's Day in the book, rather than on Christmas. Also note how the Christmas celebration extends for 12 days, not just one. Consider the foods that are eaten and the plays and events Adam and Matthew attend. Also note how the author describes people playing on ice, compared to today's ice skating or skiing. pp. 269–274)

7. What does Adam discover from Jankin? Do you think Jankin is telling the truth? *(that he lost Nick at Gorhambury two weeks before; Answers will vary. pp. 275–276)*
8. **Prediction:** Do you think Adam will go to Dame Malkin's to find Nick? If so, do you think he will find Nick there?

Supplementary Activities

1. Figurative Language: **Similes**—"shook it back like a restive horse" (p. 239); "knowledge that flared...like a flash of lighting" (p. 243); "slipped like shadows" (p. 245); "stood stock still...like baby partridges freezing among the leaves when danger approaches" (p. 245); "golden light shimmered...and stood up...like a flower stem" (p. 252); "a few people rattling around in it like a handful of dried peas in a bushel basket" (p. 267) **Personification**—"knowledge...jabbed his heart with terror" (p. 243); "wind...whistled" (p. 244); "dark creeping out of the low bushes" (p. 244); "shadows flee" (p. 245); "the river sent up an icy breath" (p. 248); "squirrel scolded him shrilly" (p. 253)
2. Music: Compose a song about something you once experienced, as Adam writes a song about his personal losses on pages 254–257.
3. Writing/Poetry: Write a poem that describes the feeling of intense disappointment Adam feels upon coming to the de Lisle house only to find it mostly empty and his father in Wales with Sir Edmund.
4. History: Research the fighting between England and Wales in 1294. What was the conflict about? Who won the conflict? *(Note that this was not a major conflict, but a response to a Welsh rebellion, which led to the building of Beaumaris Castle. By 1294, Wales was already, in reality, an English colony.)*

Chapters 21–23, pp. 277–317

Adam travels to Dame Malkin's home and finds that Nick was there, but left for Oxford with Perkin. On his way to Oxford, Adam stops to see Perkin's parents, and finds Perkin and Nick there as well. He stays to help Wat, Perkin's father, with the plowing while Perkin goes on to Oxford. Before leaving for Oxford with Nick, Adam is given new shoes, a new minstrel's surcoat and hat, and a set of bagpipes. Upon arriving at Oxford, Adam finds Perkin and is reunited with Roger who has returned earlier than expected from Wales.

Vocabulary

idling (280)
marveled (282)
intervals (283)
burly (284)
christening (285)
apothecary (287)
shrill (294)
rapturous (294)
fodder (296)
madder (300)
cobbler (300)
abruptly (301)
savage (302)
strutted (303)
meditative (307)
jostled (308)
preceded (311)
partitioned (312)
superficial (313)
vacancy (314)

Discussion Questions

1. How do Agnes and Matthew react when Adam sets out to find Nick? What does this say about them? about Adam? *(Agnes seems displeased, and Matthew is forlorn. They seem to be eager to have someone around who is entertaining and pleasant. Matthew is simply thankful to have a friend his age at the castle. It is a compliment to Adam that they appreciate his company, though students should consider if Matthew and Agnes would be as sad to see Adam go if theirs was not the only family staying at the castle. Answers will vary. p. 280)*
2. How do you think Adam feels when he doesn't find Nick at Dame Malkin's home? *(Answers will vary. Some students may think he is disappointed. Others may say he is sad, but still hopeful and happy that he knows who has Nick and how to find him. pp. 280–281)*
3. What does the state of Adam's shoes tell us about him and his long journey? *(Answers will vary. Students should note that his worn shoes indicate how long he has been traveling to find his father and his dog, and also how much he has grown since he first set out on the road with Roger. They also show readers how little money Adam has to support himself. pp. 282–283)*
4. Why do you think the author makes a point of mentioning the coming of spring? *(Answers will vary. Suggestions: The spring season indicates how long Adam has been traveling. It also may be symbolic that Adam is about to experience new beginnings after suffering so much loss. pp. 284–285)*
5. Where does Adam finally find Nick? Is this a surprise, or did you expect it? *(Adam finds Perkin at Ewelme, which means he also finds Nick there. Answers will vary. Students may note that when Adam has high hopes of finding something he lost, it often turns out differently than he had hoped. By Adam not expecting to find Perkin at his parents' house, readers probably did not expect for either Perkin or Nick to be there, either. pp. 293–294)*
6. Discuss the miller's gift to Adam. Do you think it is a good gift? Why or why not? *(Answers will vary. Point out the ease with which the miller gives away his bagpipes, which are obviously of great sentimental value to him. Discuss the difference between someone giving something when they have plenty and giving something that is in some way a sacrifice. Also note how Adam is at first disappointed in the bagpipes because playing them will keep him from singing at the same time. pp. 300–302)*
7. What does Adam learn from the Senior about the King's messenger? Of what does this remind Adam? Is Adam witnessing something significant? *(that the King's messenger was sent*

to tell people that the Parliament meeting is to include commoners from all of the cities and boroughs; the old gaffer who said great things may happen right before your eyes; Answers will vary. Note how in a monarchy, the King or Queen has complete rule, but with the introduction of the Parliament, there were more checks on monarchical power. When the role of Parliament expands to include more citizens, the model of government shifts more dramatically, and power is dispersed between more parties, giving the monarch less and less actual authority. Historically, you may note that King Edward did not intend for this extension of Parliament to remove his power, but hoped it would garner him more support among the commoners. However, the new representatives to Parliament did not always agree with the King, and he was not able to pass as many tax measures as he had hoped. pp. 311–312)

8. What are two of the four grounds of human ignorance, according to Friar Bacon? Do you agree or disagree? *(to place confidence in the opinion of the inexperienced and to hide one's lack of knowledge with superficial wisdom; Answers will vary. p. 313)*
9. When the Warden wants to see Perkin and Adam, why does Adam choose to remain with Perkin rather than go on his way? What does this say about the boys' friendship? *(Adam does not want Perkin to receive all the punishment for something they both did wrong. It shows the strength of character of both boys to face the consequences of their actions, even though they are not sure what they did wrong. It also shows the strength of their friendship that they care enough for one another to not allow their friend to suffer alone. pp. 315–316)*
10. How do you think Adam felt when he saw his father and heard him say, "You have done well, son" (p. 317)? Is that what you think Adam expected to hear? Is that what you expected Roger to say? *(Answers will vary.)*

Supplementary Activities

1. Figurative Language: **Similes**—"whole world shone and glittered like the fairy country" (p. 279); "thin as a twig" (p. 281); "bright shy eyes like a field mouse" (p. 295) **Metaphor**—Adam: young rooster (p. 312) **Personification**—"intelligent eyes" (p. 295); "cloud of gnats dancing" (p. 298)
2. Art: Draw a caricature of Adam in his brown surcoat (mantle) with his toes sticking out of his shoes, claiming to be a minstrel.
3. History: Gunnilda tries to keep witches from her cow by tying red string around its tail (p. 298). Conduct research to find other old wives' tales that people believed in the Middle Ages.

Post-reading Discussion Questions

1. Throughout the story, Adam speaks of himself as a minstrel. However, he realizes that "...at de Lisle House they did not treat him as a minstrel; to them he was a rather tiresome boy..." (p. 269). Which do you think Adam is—a mature minstrel, a tiresome boy, or both? Why? *(Answers will vary. Note that Adam does not think of himself as a boy, though he is in a constant search for his father. An adult minstrel would probably not be as concerned about being with his parent. Also note that Adam is not able to fully support himself as a minstrel apart from Roger. Before coming upon Perkin's family, he had no minstrel surcoat and no shoes that fit. He was, however, able to entertain many people, earn money to eat, and even buy a few gifts along the way.)*
2. Discuss the role of the Catholic Church in the story. How would the story have been different without being set in a religious culture? How would it have been the same? *(Answers will vary. Note how the Church officially disapproved of minstrels, though some tales were tolerated. Also note the kindnesses extended to Adam by religious people, such as Master Walter and Dame Prudence, and even the abbots at St. Alban's. Consider the many times people make religious references in their everyday talk and how the religious culture affected the morality of the day—informing even the ideas of chivalry and heroism. Also consider how many monks and abbots educated young people and how the education system in that culture was very different from today's, where the government controls education.)*
3. Why does Adam call his father "Roger" instead of "Dad" or "Father"? *(Answers will vary. One point to consider is when Adam refers to his father as Roger the minstrel in a proud way, hoping that people will recognize his father's name.)*
4. What did you learn about feudalism or patrons by reading this book? *(Answers will vary. Students may refer to understanding how workers had to serve the lord of the land before they served themselves, as in when harvest occurred. Also, students may note how Roger is bound to his patron, even to the point of going with him to a war in Wales while his son is lost, because Sir Edmund is the source of his livelihood.)*
5. If you could assume the role of any character in the novel, who would you be and why? *(Answers will vary. Encourage students to explain how they would function in that culture by taking on whichever role they choose.)*
6. Would this story be feasible in a modern-day setting? Why or why not? *(Answers will vary. Most students will say this story would not be possible today. Some reasons may include laws against children being "abandoned," modern means of travel which make walking less necessary, the lack of minstrels in today's culture, a wariness of strangers in today's world rather than a trust in them, etc.)*
7. Who are the protagonist and the antagonist in the story? How do you know? *(Adam is the protagonist, the character the reader understands and supports. Adam must overcome the obstacles before him; he is not the one causing the conflict. The antagonist is Jankin, who becomes the source of conflict when he runs away with Nick, causing Adam to lose Roger.)*
8. Would you recommend this book to a friend? Why or why not? *(Answers will vary.)*

Post-reading Extension Activities

1. In the beginning of the novel, Perkin is proud of his ability to identify various family crests. Research your own last name, and see if your family has a crest, symbol, or special meaning from long ago.
2. Design a minstrel's outfit for someone living in the Middle Ages.
3. Create a collage that shows the types of goods that would probably have been sold at a fair, such as St. Giles' Fair, in thirteenth-century England.
4. Paint or sculpt either Bayard or Nick.
5. Locate the text for one of the tales that is mentioned in the novel. Perform all or part of the tale to the class, depending on its length. Speak as you believe a minstrel would when performing.
6. Conduct research and give the class a basic lesson in how to play a harp or other string instrument.
7. At one point in the story, Adam feels left out because the other children at the de Lisle house are not paying attention to him. Write a letter to Adam giving advice on how to make friends and overcome feeling lonely.
8. Recreate the scene between Roger and Jankin at the Court of the Dusty Feet. Have the class vote on who they believe should keep Nick based on each character's arguments.
9. Just as Adam wrote a song about his hard journey, write a song Roger the minstrel might have penned while looking for his lost son and his son's beloved dog.
10. From Nick's point of view, rewrite the part of the story where Nick is stolen and chased by Adam across the river.

Assessment for *Adam of the Road*

Assessment is an ongoing process. The following ten items can be completed during the novel study. Once finished, the student and teacher will check the work. Points may be added to indicate the level of understanding.

Name ______________________________ Date ______________

Student	Teacher	
_______	_______	1. Brainstorm the pros and cons of living as a minstrel in medieval times.
_______	_______	2. Identify a major theme from the novel. Create a poster about this theme. Include quotes from the book, characters, and pictures/descriptions of events from the book to explain how the theme is evident.
_______	_______	3. Using a Venn diagram, compare and contrast Perkin and Adam.
_______	_______	4. Write a poem from Jack de Vesey's perspective discussing what it is like to live on the road. Include references to events that occur while Adam travels with him and his family.
_______	_______	5. Using the map you created in Supplementary Activity #2 (see page 18 of this guide), indicate the significant characters Adam meets at each point in his travels.
_______	_______	6. Complete the Character Web on page 9 of this guide for at least two characters in the story.
_______	_______	7. Complete the Story Map on page 10 of this guide.
_______	_______	8. Complete the Foreshadowing Chart on page 11 of this guide with at least three examples of foreshadowing used in the book.
_______	_______	9. Complete at least two of the Post-reading Extension Activities (see page 26 of this guide) and present one to the class.
_______	_______	10. Complete the Feelings chart on page 12 of this guide.

Linking Novel Units® Lessons to National and State Reading Assessments

During the past several years, an increasing number of students have faced some form of state-mandated competency testing in reading. Many states now administer state-developed assessments to measure the skills and knowledge emphasized in their particular reading curriculum. The discussion questions and post-reading questions in this Novel Units® Teacher Guide make excellent open-ended comprehension questions and may be used throughout the daily lessons as practice activities. The rubric below provides important information for evaluating responses to open-ended comprehension questions. Teachers may also use scoring rubrics provided for their own state's competency test.

Please note: The Novel Units® Student Packet contains optional open-ended questions in a format similar to many national and state reading assessments.

Scoring Rubric for Open-Ended Items

3-Exemplary	Thorough, complete ideas/information Clear organization throughout Logical reasoning/conclusions Thorough understanding of reading task Accurate, complete response
2-Sufficient	Many relevant ideas/pieces of information Clear organization throughout most of response Minor problems in logical reasoning/conclusions General understanding of reading task Generally accurate and complete response
1-Partially Sufficient	Minimally relevant ideas/information Obvious gaps in organization Obvious problems in logical reasoning/conclusions Minimal understanding of reading task Inaccuracies/incomplete response
0-Insufficient	Irrelevant ideas/information No coherent organization Major problems in logical reasoning/conclusions Little or no understanding of reading task Generally inaccurate/incomplete response